GRAMMAR WORKBOOK 5
SERIES EDITORS
JoAnn (Jodi) Crandall
Joan Kang Shin

Australia • Brazil • Mexico • Singapore • United Kingdom • United States

Unit 1

1 **Read.** Complete the sentences.

1. We just saw lightning. Next there _____'s going to_____ be thunder.

2. A sandstorm is coming. My parents _____ get the house ready.

3. It's snowing. He _____ wear a warm coat.

4. It usually rains more than this. I think there _____ be a drought.

5. It's hot today. I _____ go swimming.

2 **Read and write.** Answer the questions. Use *going to* and phrases from the box.

bring an umbrella	close all the windows	evacuate
go downstairs	~~make a snowman~~	

1. What are you going to do in the snow?

   I'm going to make a snowman.

2. What are you going to do if it's rainy?

   _____

3. How is your family going to get ready for the sandstorm?

   _____

4. Where are you going to go if there's a tornado?

   _____

5. What are your cousins going to do if there's a flood?

   _____

3 **Read and write.** Read about what's happening today. Then say that tomorrow things are going to be different.

1. Today it's really cold.

   <u>Tomorrow it's going to be hot.</u>
2. Today I'm getting up early.

   _____
3. Today my brother is staying home.

   _____
4. Today my parents aren't working.

   _____
5. Today it's raining.

   _____

4 **Read and write.** Answer with information that is true for you.

1. Is it going to rain much this week where you live?

   <u>No, but it's going to be cloudy.</u>
2. What are you <u>not</u> going to do if there's thunder and lightning?

   _____
3. What are you going to do if there's a flood?

   _____
4. If you have to evacuate your house, where are you going to go?

   _____

5 **Write.** There's no school because of a blizzard. Write four things you're going to do today.

_____

_____

_____

_____

GRAMMAR

If it **rains**, I **take** an umbrella.

If there **is** a tornado, then we **go** to a shelter.

If a blizzard **comes**, my family **stays** inside.

If the lights **go out**, they **use** a torch.

1 **Read.** Circle the correct answer.

1. **If there / There's** is an emergency, we follow our plan.

2. If it rains, then **if I use / I use** an umbrella.

3. If a tornado comes, **if we evacuate / we evacuate**.

4. If Jon knows it's going to be cold, he **wears / wore** his coat and gloves.

5. **Is / If** it's hot, we go swimming.

6. If **there / there's** a blizzard, we don't have school.

2 **Read and write.** Complete the sentences.

1. If it's hurricane season, it rains a lot.

2. If it snows, _____

3. If the electricity goes out, _____

4. If a blizzard comes, _____

5. If there's no rain for weeks, _____

6. If there's a flood in my town, _____

4

3 **Read and write.** Complete the sentences with a phrase beginning with *if.*

1. <u>If there's a blizzard</u>, people can't drive.

2. _____, we need a torch.

3. _____, I make an emergency plan.

4. _____, I call my parents.

5. _____, people evacuate.

6. _____, we go to a storm shelter.

4 **Read and write.** Answer the questions in complete sentences.

1. What do people wear if it rains?

   <u>If it rains, people wear raincoats.</u>

2. What do you do if it snows?

   _____

3. What does your family do if a tornado comes?

   _____

4. What do dogs do if there is a heat wave?

   _____

5 **Write.** Write five sentences using the phrases in the box and *if.*

| be very windy | feel cold | hear about a tornado on the radio |
| miss the bus | ~~see a lion~~ | see thunder and lightning |

<u>If I see a lion, I run.</u>

_____

_____

_____

_____

Unit 2

1 **Read.** Circle the correct answer.

1. A cheetah is **faster than** / **as fast** as an elephant.

2. An elephant is **larger than** / **as large as** a horse.

3. An poisonous spider is **more dangerous than** / **as dangerous as** a poisonous snake.

4. Zebras are about **as big as** / **much bigger than** horses.

5. A bee is **smaller than** / **as small as** a salamander.

2 **Read and write.** Compare using *as . . . as* and the words in parentheses.

1. A deer is not _____ (fast) a jaguar.

2. Otters can be _____ (playful) monkeys.

3. Some frogs are _____ (poisonous) snakes.

4. Donkeys are not _____ (beautiful) horses.

5. An elephant is not _____ (loud) a lion.

6. An alligator's skin is not _____ (smooth) a seal's skin.

3 **Read and write.** Compare using *(not) as . . . as.*

1. A bee's sting can be dangerous, but a poisonous spider's bite is more dangerous!

   A bee's sting is not as dangerous as a poisonous spider's bite.

2. My sister thinks baby seals are really cute. She thinks lion cubs are really cute, too!

   _____

3. Cheetahs can run at a speed of around 110 kph (68 mph). Sailfish can swim at 110 kph.

   _____

4. A baby elephant is big! It weighs about 90 kg (200 lb.), the same as two small people.

   _____

4 **Write.** Compare using *(not) as . . . as.*

1. insect / leaf

   <u>Some insects are as green as a leaf.</u>

2. cat's fur / rabbit's fur

   _____

3. seal / elephant

   _____

4. snakes / crocodiles

   _____

5. baby seal / baby otter

   _____

5 **Write.** Write five sentences comparing yourself to people just like you.

<u>I am as old as my cousin Jack.</u>

_____

_____

_____

_____

1 **Read.** Circle the letter.

1. Some species look like others, _____?

   a. do they   b. don't they   c. aren't they

2. Copycat animals are amazing, _____?

   a. isn't they   b. don't they   c. aren't they

3. Those deer weren't running from a lion, _____?

   a. were they   b. aren't they   c. weren't they

4. Donkeys are funny animals, _____?

   a. can't they   b. aren't they   c. are they

2 **Read and write.** Complete the questions.

1. Some insects are poisonous, _____?

2. Camouflage doesn't help all animals hide, _____?

3. Those fish swim fast, _____?

4. That frog had stripes, _____?

5. A cheetah can run faster than a human, _____?

6. A predator is dangerous to its prey, _____?

7. Those animals won't imitate any other species, _____?

8. The dog we saw yesterday wasn't very nice, _____?

3 **Look and write.** Ask a question about each animal.

1. <u>This butterfly is beautiful, isn't it?</u>

2. _____

3. _____

4. _____

5. _____

6. _____

4 **Write.** Write four questions to ask your friend about this week's events.

<u>The game we played after school was fun, wasn't it?</u>

_____

_____

_____

_____

Unit 3

1 **Read and match.** Draw a line.

1. Has she ever sung in a band?   a. No, I never have.

2. Have you ever danced at a concert?   b. Yes, she has.

3. Have they ever played music together?   c. No, we never have.

4. Has he seen his favourite band play?   d. Yes, they have.

5. Have we ever been in band class together?   e. No, he never has.

2 **Read.** Complete the sentences with *ever* or *never*.

1. I have _____never_____ played this instrument before.

2. I have _____ seen your violin before.

3. This will be the first time I have _____ played that song.

4. Have you _____ been in an orchestra?

5. My parents have _____ heard this band play.

6. I have _____ felt both so nervous and so excited before.

7. Have you _____ seen such unusual instruments?

8. No, we _____ have.

3 **Read and write.** Answer the questions in complete sentences.

1. Have you ever played the saxophone?

   <u>No, I have never played the saxophone.</u>

2. Have you ever had guitar lessons?

   _____

3. Have you ever written a song?

   _____

4. Have your friends ever heard you sing?

   _____

5. Have you ever met a famous musician? If so, who?

   _____

4 **Write.** Write questions with the words. Then answer them in complete sentences.

1. flute

   <u>Have you ever played a flute?</u>

   <u>Yes, I have played the flute.</u>

2. drums

   _____

   _____

3. concert

   _____

   _____

4. lead singer

   _____

   _____

5 **Write.** Write two interesting things you have done. Write two things you have never done.

<u>I have seen a Chinese opera.</u>

_____

GRAMMAR

I play the bass guitar **better than** I play the drums.

My brother learns **as easily as** I do.

He practises **less often than** I do.

She listens to jazz **more often than** she listens to hip-hop.

The neighbours turn on the radio **more loudly than** we do.

I sing **worse than** you do.

1 **Read.** Circle the best answer.

1. I like pop music **more well** / **better** than I like rock.

2. He can't sing very well. He sings **worse** / **less better** than I do.

3. Like me, my sister practises the piano every day. She practises **harder** / **as hard as** I do.

4. My dad sings **more loudly** / **as loudly** than anyone else in the family.

5. When he dances, his feet move **faster than** / **less fast** mine.

6. She plays the piano on Sundays, but I play every day. She plays **better** / **less often** than I do.

2 **Write.** Complete the sentences.

1. I like being in the jazz band _____as well as_____ (=, well) being in the orchestra.

2. She can play the violin _____ (+, well) she can play the piano.

3. He listens to classical music _____ (-, often) he listens to rock.

4. Do you sing _____ (=, badly) your sister?

5. When my dad plays the guitar, his hands move _____ (+, fast) mine do.

6. He plays the guitar _____ (=, often) he plays the drums.

3 **Write.** Use the words to write comparative sentences.

1. he / sing / =, well / sister

   He sings as well as his sister (does).

2. she / practise the piano / -, often / brother

   _____

3. she / play flute / +, beautifully / her teacher

   _____

4. rock music / sound / +, fast / classical music

   _____

5. musicians / play / drums / +, loudly / violin

   _____

6. I / do ballet / =, well / do hip-hop dancing

   _____

4 **Read and write.** Answer the questions using comparatives.

1. What do you listen to more often — rock or hip-hop?

   I listen to hip-hop more often than I listen to rock.

2. Who sings better — you or your best friend?

   _____

3. What do you do as well as your parents?

   _____

4. What do you play more often — sports or music?

   _____

5. Think of your two favourite bands. Which one do you like better?

   _____

Units 1–3: Review

1 **Read and match.** Draw a line.

1. Is it going to snow?   a. If there's a sandstorm, I stay inside.

2. Is it going to be warm tomorrow?   b. Yes, there's going to be a blizzard.

3. I see wind moving the sand.   c. If it gets hot, I go to the pool.

4. A heat wave is coming.   d. No, it's going to be cool and windy.

2 **Read and write.** Complete the sentences.

1. A monkey will climb ___higher than___ (+, high) a panda, ___won't it___?

2. Some wasps are _____ (=, poisonous) snakes, _____?

3. An otter can swim _____ (+, well) a dog, _____?

4. A cheetah runs _____ (+, fast) its prey, _____?

3 **Read and write.** Complete the dialogue.

CAMILO: Have you _____ to a sanctuary for big cats? It's like a zoo for
tigers, lions and other wild cats.

ALMA: No, I _____.

CAMILO: Sounds cool, _____?

ALMA: Yes, it does! Was it _____ it sounds?

CAMILO: Even cooler! I loved all the cats. I even got to feed one of them!

ALMA: Wow! Sounds great. I'm _____ do something cool, too. I'm

_____ see my first jazz concert! Have you _____ to
a concert?

CAMILO: Yes, _____. My dad plays the trumpet. _____ he has
a concert, we go to see him.

4 Look and write.

1.

There's going to be a tornado.

If there's a tornado, we go to a shelter.

2.

_____

_____

3.

_____

_____

4.

_____

_____

5 Write. Respond with complete sentences.

1. Have you ever seen a cheetah? _____

_____

2. Compare a cheetah to another animal. _____

_____

3. Have you ever played an instrument? Which one? _____

_____

4. If you're at a concert, what do you do? _____

_____

Unit 4

GRAMMAR

Other planets **may/might** have oxygen.

I <u>think</u> that light in the sky **may** be a planet.

We <u>know</u> there **may/might** be extraterrestrials in another galaxy.

We **may/might** see another comet soon.

I <u>thought</u> that light in the sky **might** be a planet.

We <u>knew</u> there **might** be extraterrestrials in another galaxy.

1 **Read and match.** Draw a line.

1. What star is that?

2. Is there life on other planets?

3. What was that shape moving in the sky?

4. Will extraterrestrials visit Earth?

a. There might be.

b. It may be the North Star.

c. They may.

d. I thought it might be a comet.

2 **Read and write.** Complete the sentences with *may* or *might*.

1. We think Jupiter _____may/might_____ be the biggest planet in our solar system.

2. I thought that we _____ have gone back to the moon by now.

3. One day people _____ be able to go to space on holiday.

4. The astronauts _____ have to be in space for many months.

5. He _____ go to space camp one day.

6. She didn't agree that there _____ be life in other galaxies.

7. They knew that the big star in the sky _____ be a planet.

8. Have you heard there _____ be a new planet in our solar system?

3 **Read and write.** Use words from the box and *may* or *might*.

be	come	have	see	~~try~~	win

1. They thought extraterrestrials _____might try_____ to contact us.

2. Scientists say that a comet _____ close to Earth in a few years.

3. We thought that the film about life on other planets _____ the prize for best picture.

4. There _____ more galaxies than we know in the universe.

5. We thought scientists _____ water on Mars.

4 **Read and write.** Answer the questions with your own ideas. Use *may* or *might*.

1. Is there a planet that doesn't have a moon?

   There might *be a planet that doesn't have a moon.*

2. How long will it take to receive a message from extraterrestrials?

   _____

3. When will we next see a comet in the sky?

   _____

4. Do plants and animals live on other planets?

   _____

5. How many galaxies are there?

   _____

5 **Look and write.** Imagine this is a new planet. Write three sentences about it. Use *may* or *might*.

There might *be trees on this planet.*

_____

_____

_____

GRAMMAR

Jon, Paolo and Ana all want to learn about the stars.	**Everyone** wants to learn about the stars.
Jon, Paolo or Ana can be a scientist.	**Anyone** can be a scientist.
Ana is funny.	**Someone** is funny.
Jon, Paolo and Ana aren't astronauts.	**No one** is an astronaut.

1 **Read.** Match the word that can replace each underlined phrase. Draw a line.

1. <u>All the students in my class</u> want to fly to the moon.   a. no one

2. Did you talk to <u>any of the astronauts who visited school</u>?   b. everyone

3. My phone is ringing. <u>Another person</u> is trying to call me.   c. anyone

4. <u>None of the people who live here</u> are at home.   d. someone

2 **Read.** Circle the correct answer.

1. Outer space is really interesting! **Everyone** / **No one** is interested in space, aren't they?

2. **No one** / **Someone** from another planet might try to communicate with us. Don't be surprised if you hear about it one day.

3. Most people don't believe there's life on other planets. Does **everyone** / **anyone** think extraterrestrials are out there?

4. I want to believe in extraterrestrials, but really there's **no one** / **anyone** out there.

5. We were all invited to see the stars with a scientist. I'd like **no one** / **everyone** in the group to go.

6. **Someone** / **Anyone** is coming to speak to our class. I think it might be an astronomer.

3 **Read and write.** Complete the paragraph. Use *anyone, everyone, no one* and *someone.*

Not _____ says that there is life on other planets. Do you think

_____ is out there that's as intelligent as humans? Some people say there's

_____ out there at all. Others definitely say that there's life on other

planets. Do you know _____ who says they have seen an extraterrestrial?

I want to say that _____ is out there, but I might not really believe

_____ who said they saw an extraterrestrial.

4 **Read and write.** Rewrite the sentences. Use *anyone, everyone, no one* and *someone.*

1. All the students in my class went to the science centre.

   Everyone went to the science centre.

2. The teacher asked if any of the students knew all the planets.

   _____

3. One student could name all of them.

   _____

4. I knew that none of the students could name the comets.

   _____

5. We all learnt a lot about our solar system.

   _____

5 **Look and write.** Write three questions and answers. Use *anyone, everyone, no one* and *someone.*

Is anyone playing the violin? No, no one is playing the violin.

_____

_____

_____

Unit 5

1 **Write.** Change each word to the *-ing* form.

1. tell _____

2. listen _____

3. weave _____

4. play _____

5. create _____

6. share _____

2 **Read and write.**

1. ____Reading____ (read) my grandparents' old letters is cool.

2. _____ (cook) with my grandmother is one of my favourite things to do.

3. _____ (know) family traditions helps me understand my culture.

4. _____ (share) stories is a regular activity in my family.

3 **Read and write.**

In my family, _____ (keep) our culture strong over generations is very

important. _____ (cook) and _____ (eat) traditional foods is

one way my family has held on to traditions. _____ (tell) stories is another way

we share our family's history. _____ (teach) my brothers and sisters and I about

our culture is something my parents and grandparents care about. But they don't just talk —

they show us what our ancestors did. For example, _____ (make) artwork and

_____ (weave) cloth are two of our ancestors' activities that we've learnt to do.

4 **Look and write.** Use the *-ing* form.

1. _____ with your family is really important.

2. _____ can be really fun.

3. _____ is a good way to make friends.

4. _____ is an important tradition in many cultures.

5 **Write.** Choose four activities or use your own. Write about your family's traditions.

cook	eat	play traditional music
read	share	storytell
take photos	talk	visit

Eating together is something my family likes doing every day.

_____

_____

_____

_____

GRAMMAR

I like **sharing** my culture with new friends.

She is excited about **visiting** her relatives.

My grandmother is good at **embroidering** clothes.

My cousin enjoys **dancing** to traditional music.

1 **Read and write.** Complete the sentences.

1. She likes _____ (make) jewellery.

2. They enjoy _____ (learn) about their family's traditions.

3. I am good at _____ (create) handcrafted items.

4. Are you interested in _____ (share) something about your culture?

5. My grandfather likes _____ (tell) stories about his friends.

6. We enjoy _____ (play) games together as a family.

7. They are excited about _____ (dance) for the tourists.

8. I enjoy _____ (eat) foods from other cultures.

2 **Unscramble.** Then circle the sentences that are true for you.

1. culture / eating / enjoy / I / foods / my / from

   I enjoy eating foods from my culture.

2. taking / I / my / family / like / pictures / of

   _____

3. fun / is / my / hands / making / things / with

   _____

4. interested / in / I'm / creating / pottery / not

   _____

5. my / hobby / grandma / weaving / with / is / my / favourite

   _____

3 **Look and write.**

1. They enjoy _____ as a way to tell stories.

2. The boy is interested in _____ music with his grandfather.

3. She is very good at _____ pottery.

4. We really like _____ our hands to make sculptures.

4 **Read and write.** Answer the questions.

1. Think of a person in your family. What activity does this person enjoy doing?

_____

2. What handicrafts are you interested in doing?

_____

3. What sport or game do you most enjoy playing with your friends?

_____

4. What are you really good at?

_____

5 **Write.** What do you enjoy doing at school? What are you interested in? What are you good at? Write three sentences.

_____

_____

_____

Unit 6

GRAMMAR

Some plants **are grown** in a greenhouse.

Water **is used** to help plants grow.

A fly **is digested** by the Venus flytrap.

How **are** flies **tricked** by the stink lily?

They **are attracted** to its smell.

1 **Read.** Circle the correct answer.

1. Nutrients **eat / are eaten** by a plant's roots.

2. The seed is **carries / carried** away by a bird.

3. Dragon blood trees are **found / find** on islands in the Indian Ocean.

4. Bees **attract / are attracted** by the pollen on some plants.

2 **Write.** Unscramble the sentences. Look at p. 94 in your Student's Book.

1. are / found / desert / the / Socotra / dragon blood trees / in / of

   Dragon blood trees are found in the desert of Socotra.

2. shaped / is / the / like / tree / an / foot / elephant's

   _____

3. are / dragon blood trees / used / make / to / medicine

   _____

4. also / desert/ found / is / desert rose / the / in / the

   _____

3 Read and write. Complete the sentences with the correct form of the words from the box.

| attract | catch | eat | ~~find~~ | need | pick | plant |

1. Some interesting plants _____*are found*_____ in the rainforest.

2. The rain there _____ to help plants grow.

3. Sometimes flowers _____ from these plants.

4. Plants _____ by animals as well as people.

5. Insects _____ to plants that can eat them.

6. Flies _____ inside the Venus flytrap's leaves.

4 Read and write. Answer the questions.

1. What do plants need for survival?

   Light, air, water and nutrients _____

2. How does the Venus flytrap attract flies?

   _____ the Venus flytrap's sweet smell.

3. Where can you find cacti?

   _____ in deserts.

5 Write. Write three sentences about what's done in your classroom each day. Use the words from the box or your own.

| give | hear | make | read | see | speak | write |

Homework is given by the teacher. _____

_____

_____

GRAMMAR

I like flowers **that** smell sweet.

The Venus flytrap is a flower **that** can eat insects.

Daisies have a yellow centre **that** attracts bees.

Do you see the vine **that** grows around the tree?

1 **Read and write.** Complete the sentences.

1. The *Rafflesia arnoldii* is a plant ____that smells____ (smell) like rotting meat.

2. Daisies are flowers _____ (have) yellow centres and white petals.

3. The *Hydnora africana* is a strange plant _____ (look) like a mouth.

4. Most plants have roots _____ (grow) under the ground.

5. The sensitive plant is a plant _____ (move) when someone touches it.

6. It has tiny leaves _____ (close) up under your finger.

2 **Read.** *That* is missing in five places. Write *that* where it belongs. The first one is done for you.

Meat-eating plants like the Venus flytrap are special plants ^that^ grow in places don't have the things most plants need for survival. For example, the soil where these plants grow may not have the nutrients needed. Such plants have found new ways to live and grow.

Like the Venus flytrap, the pitcher plant is a plant eats insects. Insects are attracted to the top of the plant, the part has the brightest colours. Then the insect is trapped by tiny hairs grow inside the plant.

3 **Read and write.** Complete the sentences. Use *that* and information from the box.

> carry / nutrients and water
>
> climb / walls and trees
>
> feel / sharp
>
> have / white petals
>
> look like / eyes
>
> ~~smell / nice~~

1. The rose is a flower that smells nice. _____

2. Vines are plants _____

3. The white baneberry has fruit _____

4. Daisies are simple flowers _____

5. The root is the part of the plant _____

6. The thorn is the part of the rose that _____

4 **Write.** Write five sentences to describe your favourite animals. Use *that* in your sentences.

Leopards are animals that have spots. _____

_____

_____

_____

_____

_____

Units 4–6: Review

1 **Read.** Circle the correct answer.

1. I didn't think **anyone / no one** would buy the handicrafts that I made.

   Right, but your mum thought that someone **may / might**, didn't she?

2. Do you think **no one / anyone** will appreciate the flower garden I planted?

   Of course! **Everyone / Anyone** loves gardens! Especially gardens

   that have / having flowers.

3. Do you think **someone / everyone** else might live out in space?

   Maybe. **Finding / Find** extraterrestrials in our galaxy is something that

   everyone / no one has ever done.

2 **Read.** Circle the letter.

1. _____ is one way to pass traditions down from one generation to another.

   a. Tell stories   b. Storytelling   c. That tell stories

2. My aunt really enjoys _____ daisies and roses in her garden.

   a. is grown   b. might grow   c. growing

3. An insect that lands on a Venus flytrap _____ by the plant.

   a. might be digested   b. may digest   c. digesting

4. _____ can make pottery. It's not that difficult!

   a. No one   b. Anyone   c. Someone

5. There _____ be some new sculptures in the mueum.

   a. may   b. that   c. are made

6. Extraterrestrials _____ on many other planets, aren't they?

   a. find   b. are found   c. that find

3 Read and write.

1. Scientists study stars through a telescope. _Stars are studied (by scientists)_

   through a telescope.

2. Ancestors pass on traditions across generations. _____

   _____

3. Rocks, ice and gas make up a comet. _____

4. The smell of rotting meat attracts insects to plants. _____

   _____

5. People use a wheel to make pottery. _____

4 Write. Use *that* in complete sentences.

1. rose / flower / long stem

   A rose is a flower that has a long stem.

2. sunflower / flower / yellow petals

   _____

3. astronaut / person / space

   _____

4. Venus flytrap / plant / insect

   _____

5. weaving / handicraft / ancestors

   _____

5 Write. Complete the sentences.

1. Playing _piano is my mum's favourite thing to do._

2. Reading _____

3. I enjoy _____

4. My friends are interested in _____

5. Doing homework _____

6. My parents are good at _____

Unit 7

GRAMMAR

If the volcano **erupts**, everything **will burn**.

If everything **burns**, animals **won't have** a place to live.

won't = will not

Everything **will burn if** the volcano **erupts**.

Animals **won't have** a place to live **if** everything burns.

1 **Read.** Circle the correct answer.

1. If a volcano **will erupt** / **erupts**, animals **will run** / **run** away.

2. A volcano **forms** / **will form** if magma **will push** / **pushes** up the earth's crust.

3. It **will be** / **is** difficult to breathe if gases **will blast** / **blast** into the sky.

4. If lava **will touch** / **touches** anything, it **will burn** / **burns**.

2 **Read and write.** Complete the sentences.

1. People who live near an active volcano _____won't be_____ (be) safe if it erupts.

2. If scientists visit a volcano, they _____ (collect) some ash.

3. If ash fills the air, the sky _____ (be) blue.

4. You _____ (see) a volcano called Mauna Loa if you go to Hawaii.

3 **Read and write.** Complete the sentences.

1. I will put a raincoat on if it rains _____.

2. If you plant some seeds, _____.

3. _____ if he sees a comet.

4. Lava will cover the ground _____.

5. If there's a tornado, _____.

6. _____ if there's a blizzard.

30

4 **Look and write.** Write a sentence about each picture. Use *if* and *will*.

1.   If the dog sees a cat, it will jump on it.

2.   _____

3.   _____

4.   _____

5 **Write.** Write a sentence about each of the topics. Use *if* and *will* in your sentences.

extreme weather	family	hobbies
school	sports	wild animals

If I visit my grandparents this summer, we will look at old photographs.

_____

_____

_____

_____

_____

GRAMMAR

Because of the lava, everything burnt.	Everything burnt **because of** the lava.
Because of the pressure, the magma exploded.	The magma exploded **because of** the pressure.
Because of the ash, no one could see the crater.	No one could see the crater **because of** the ash.

1 **Read.** Circle the letter of the logical statement in each pair.

1. a. We were in a storm shelter because of the tornado.

   b. There was a tornado because we were in a storm shelter.

2. a. Because school was cancelled, there was a snowstorm.

   b. School was cancelled because of a snowstorm.

3. a. Because we ran up the hill, there were big waves.

   b. We ran up the hill because of the big waves.

4. a. Because we drank lots of water, it was hot.

   b. We drank lots of water because of the heat.

2 **Unscramble.** Add commas as needed.

1. studied / the test / I / because / last night / of

   <u>Because of the test, I studied last night. / I studied last night because of the test.</u>

2. many / people / the / eruption / of / their / homes / because / left

   _____

3. of / because / I / the / cold / blankets / put / on

   _____

4. because / dried / up / the / drought / the / flowers / of

   _____

5. of / the / hurricane / from / the / water / the / animals / because / ran

   _____

3 **Look and write.** Complete the sentences.

1. 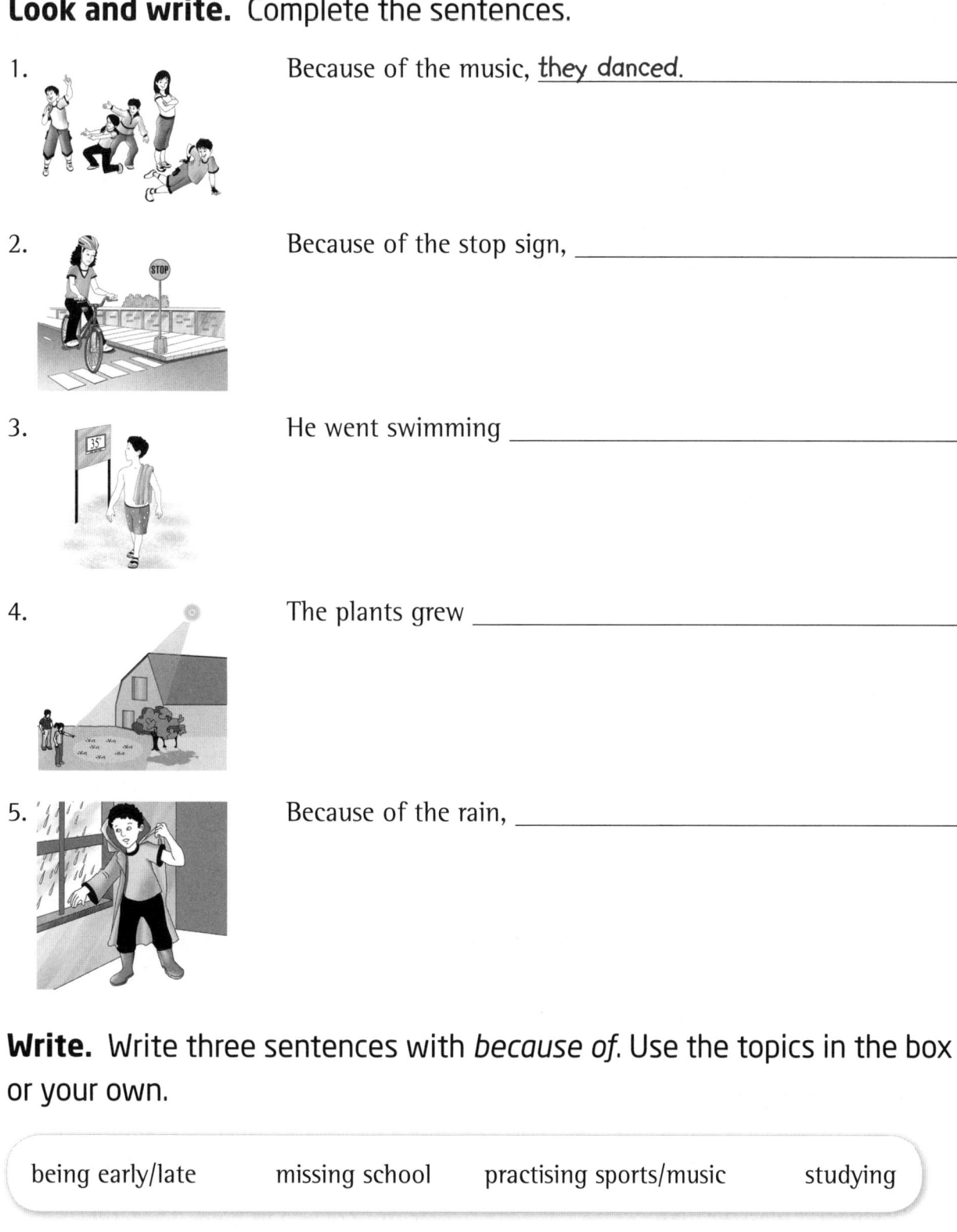   Because of the music, <u>they danced.</u> _____

2.   Because of the stop sign, _____

3.   He went swimming _____

4.   The plants grew _____

5.   Because of the rain, _____

4 **Write.** Write three sentences with *because of*. Use the topics in the box or your own.

> being early/late   missing school   practising sports/music   studying

<u>Because of my broken alarm clock, I woke up late.</u> _____

_____

_____

_____

Unit 8

1 **Read.** Circle the sentence with a similar meaning.

1. The broken sink must be mended to conserve water.

   a. Somebody has to mend the broken sink to conserve water.

   b. We can conserve water with the broken sink.

2. Green shopping bags must be used to help reduce waste.

   a. Everyone should use green shopping bags to reduce waste.

   b. We must reduce waste from green shopping bags.

3. Energy can be conserved by turning off the lights.

   a. We must always leave the lights off.

   b. We use less energy when we turn off the lights.

4. Some chemicals may be kept in special bottles.

   a. People shouldn't put some chemicals in bottles.

   b. It's possible to keep some chemicals in special bottles.

2 **Read and write.**

In order to save the environment, glass and plastic _must be recycled_ (must / recycle).

Plastic and glass bottles _____ (can / collect) in bags. Then they

_____ (can / take) to a recycling centre. These bottles also _____

(can / reuse) in many creative ways. Plastic bottles _____ (can / use) to make

fleece jackets. Glass bottles _____ (can / clean) with soap and water. Then they

_____ (may / fill) with water and flowers for a beautiful decoration!

34

3 **Write.** Use *can, must* or *may* in your sentences.

1. plants / grow / farms

Plants can *be grown on farms.*

2. rubbish / put / landfill sites

_____

3. green bags / bring / shop

_____

4. the environment / protect

_____

5. everything / reuse / creatively

_____

4 **Write.** Use the words with *can, must* or *may* to write about the objects in the photo.

1. use Cardboard can *be used to make art.*

2. recycle _____

3. reuse _____

4. put _____

5. make _____

5 **Write.** Write three things that *can, must* or *may* be done at your school to protect the environment.

We can reuse paper in our classroom.

_____

_____

_____

GRAMMAR

When we have short showers, we conserve water.

We conserve water **when we have short showers**.

When we pick up rubbish, we help keep our environment beautiful.

We help keep our environment beautiful **when we pick up rubbish**.

1 **Read.** Rewrite the sentences. Add commas if necessary.

1. We reduce our water use when we collect rainwater.

   When we collect rainwater, we reduce our water use.

2. When we reuse shopping bags, we reduce our use of plastic.

   _____

3. We reduce waste when we recycle plastic bottles.

   _____

4. When we recycle, we show that we care about the environment.

   _____

2 **Read and write.** Use phrases from the box.

> make art   recycle metal   ~~have long showers~~
> throw away plastic   work together

1. We waste water when we have long showers _____.

2. _____, it sits in landfill sites for a long time.

3. We save energy _____ instead of making new metal.

4. _____ from junk, we are being creative.

5. _____, we can better protect the environment.

3 **Look and write.** Complete the sentences.

1. When we turn the temperature down, <u>we conserve energy.</u>

2. We are protecting the environment _____

    _____

3. _____,

    we can harm animals living in the water.

4. _____, you can harm the

    environment.

4 **Write.** Complete the sentences.

1. When I am playing _____ (sport), _____

2. I am happy when _____

3. When I have a test, _____

4. I get excited when _____

5. When I hear my favourite song, _____

5 **Write.** How do you protect the environment? Write two sentences with *when*.

<u>When I drink a bottle of water, I recycle the bottle.</u>

_____

_____

Unit 9

1 **Read and match.** Draw a line.

1. If we stayed at a big hotel,

2. You would have so much fun

3. If I stay at the hotel near the beach,

4. We will need passports

5. We'd go to Greece

a. if you visited a theme park.

b. I'll swim in the sea every day.

c. if we fly to another country.

d. if my parents liked history more.

e. we would eat breakfast in its restaurant.

2 **Read and write.** Complete the sentences.

1. If they went on holiday this summer, they ____would go____ (go) somewhere on a ship.

2. They _____ (learn) more about their ancestors if they visited their grandparents.

3. If I liked adventure, I _____ (try) mountain climbing.

4. If they didn't love water, they _____ (not stay) at a water park.

5. _____ (take) photos if a tour guide showed you some ruins?

3 **Read and write.** Complete the sentences.

If I went on holiday, I _____ (not go) to a theme park. I love history, so I'd want to go to a country with an interesting history. For example, if I _____ (spend) time in Greece, I _____ (be) so excited. If I _____ (go) to Athens, I _____ (see) all the ruins at the Acropolis. If I _____ (have) time, I _____ (take) pictures at all of the sites. Of course, my mum _____ (want) to go shopping in the city if we _____ (can). After, if we felt very tired, we _____ (not visit) the museums. Instead, we _____ (sit) on the beach and relax.

4 **Look and write.** Use *if* and *would* in your sentences.

1. (see / take) <u>If I saw lions, I'd take a picture.</u>

2. (play / wet) _____

3. (go camping / sleep) _____

4. (stay resort / swim) _____

   _____

5 **Write.** Imagine your teacher is planning a class trip. Write two sentences about it using *if* and *would*.

<u>If we went on a safari, we would learn about the animals.</u>

_____

_____

GRAMMAR

They'**d rather see** wildlife **than see** ruins.

I'**d rather go** swimming **than go** hiking.

Would he **rather wear** sunglasses **or wear** a hat?

He'**d rather wear** a hat **than wear** sunglasses.

I'**d rather not stay** at this hotel.

I'd = I would

He'd = He would

They'd = They would

1 **Read.** Complete the sentences with *rather* and/or *than*.

1. He would _____ fly _____ take a boat.

2. Would they _____ buy souvenirs _____ see the sites?

3. I would _____ see animals at the zoo _____ go on safari.

4. He'd _____ not come with us.

5. Would she _____ go to the hotel _____ go dancing?

6. My parents are planning a holiday, but they'd _____ keep it a surprise.

2 **Read and write.** Complete the sentences.

1. I ____would rather swim____ in the sea ____than swim____ in a lake. (swim)

2. She _____ seafood _____ meat. (eat)

3. _____ get exercise on your holiday? (relax)

4. He _____ to the beach _____ to a water park. (go)

5. We _____ by train _____ by bus. (go)

3 **Write.** Ask questions with *would* and *rather.*

1. your best friend / go sightseeing / go hiking

   <u>Would your best friend rather go sightseeing than go hiking?</u>

2. you and your family / go on a tour of the city / go shopping

   _____

3. your mother / travel by ship / fly in an aeroplane

   _____

4. you / visit a museum / go to the zoo

   _____

4 **Read and write.** Answer the questions in Activity 3.

1. <u>My best friend would rather go hiking than go sightseeing.</u>

2. _____

3. _____

4. _____

5 **Read and write.** Your friend sent you a text message about the weekend. You don't like the activities he describes. Write a text back saying what you'd rather do.

> Hi! I really want to study for maths on Saturday morning. I'd also like to help my sister clean the house. Then let's go out for hamburgers. On Sunday you can come and visit my grandparents with me if you'd like! Please tell me if this is OK.

<u>I'd rather play a game than study for maths.</u>

_____

_____

_____

_____

_____

Units 7–9: Review

1 Read. Circle the letter.

1. When we turn off the lights, _____.

   a. we conserve electricity   b. rather than conserve electricity

2. If you stayed at this hotel, _____ in the big pool.

   a. you will swim   b. you would swim

3. When we buy renewable materials, _____.

   a. we protect the earth   b. we protected the earth

4. When the bottles are empty, they _____.

   a. would recycle   b. can be recycled

5. He would rather go to the beach _____ at the water park.

   a. if he swam   b. than swim

2 Read and write. Complete the predictions.

1. If plastic bottles go to a landfill site, they ____will stay____ (stay) there for a long time.

2. If I _____ (visit) my friends, we will talk for hours.

3. We _____ (see) The Great Wall if we travel to China.

4. Lava will burn you if you _____ (touch) it.

5. If my parents go on holiday, they _____ (buy) me a souvenir.

3 Read and write. Answer the questions.

1. Should I keep the chemicals on the floor?

   no / may be No, the chemicals may be kept on a shelf. _____

2. Should we make some art from these old cans?

   yes / can be _____

3. Should we throw away the plastic bottles?

42   no / must be _____

4 **Write.** Use words from each column with *if* and *would*.

I	have enough money	relax in bed
my brother/sister	have too much homework	run very fast
my parents	lose electricity	get wet
my classmates and I	see a volcano erupt	talk to my teacher
	stay at a nice hotel	go on a safari
	visit a water park	use a torch
		swim in the pool

1. If I stayed at a nice hotel, I'd swim in the pool.

2. _____

3. _____

4. _____

5. _____

5 **Write.** Write questions. Then answer them.

1. see wildlife in a zoo / on a safari

Question: Would you rather see wildlife in a zoo than on a safari?

Answer: _____

2. hike up a volcano / fly over a volcano

Question: _____

Answer: _____

3. go camping / stay at a resort

Question: _____

Answer: _____

6 **Write.** Use *because of* to explain three environmental problems.

Because of plastic bags, the ocean is polluted.

_____

_____

_____

Units 1-9: Review

1 Read. Circle the letter.

1. The teacher said that a poisonous frog _____ as dangerous as a cobra.

   a. might be   b. would rather be   c. that is

2. Betsy _____ heard this song before.

   a. has ever   b. has never   c. have ever

3. This hotel is really beautiful, _____?

   a. is it   b. it isn't   c. isn't it

4. If I knew a volcano was active, I _____ near it.

   a. won't go   b. wouldn't go   c. go

5. If I practise the flute, I _____ in the spring concert.

   a. can be played   b. will play   c. would play

6. You don't believe that there are extraterrestials in outer space, _____?

   a. aren't there   b. don't you   c. do you

2 Read and match. Draw a line.

1. A rose is a flower   a. the land is covered with lava and ash.

2. Flies are attracted to this plant   b. I would rather reuse them.

3. Instead of throwing cans away,   c. that has a stem with thorns.

4. Dad thinks   d. there may be interesting ruins near here.

5. I thought   e. it would be very scary.

6. When a volcano erupts,   f. recycling old objects into art.

7. If a volcano erupted near my house,   g. because of its sweet smell.

8. I really enjoy   h. our family might go to the beach this
                                            summer.

44

3 Read. Circle the correct answer.

1. If I make some traditional food, I **will** / **would** share it with my friends.

2. She **will** / **would** stay in a resort on the beach if she went to the Caribbean.

3. We **stay** / **would stay** inside when we hear thunder and lightning.

4. If people recycled more, there **is** / **would be** less rubbish in landfill sites.

4 Read and write. Change the form of the words in the box.

| attract |
| eat |
| paint |
| stay |

1. _____ safe in a storm is important.

2. The Venus flytrap is good at _____ insects and then _____ them.

3. _____ is my mother's favourite hobby. She's very artistic!

5 Write. Rewrite the sentence.

1. Volcanoes attract many tourists to the area.

   <u>Many tourists are attracted to the area by the volcanoes.</u>

2. Musicians play the melody quietly.

   _____

3. The idea of extraterrestials interests many scientists.

   _____

4. Everyone must carry umbrellas when it rains.

   _____

6 Read and write. Answer the questions with *going to*. Replace the underlined words.

1. Will <u>all the tourists</u> on the safari see the wildlife?

   Yes, <u>everyone on the safari is going to see the wildlife.</u>

2. Will <u>a member of your family</u> share stories about your past with you?

   Yes, _____

3. Will <u>any of the scientists</u> touch a poisonous frog?

   No, _____

7 **Look and write.** Make comparisons about the photos.

1. (=, fast) _____

_____

2. (+, bad) _____

_____

3. (–, often) _____

_____

8 **Read and write.** Answer the questions in complete sentences.

1. Have you ever thrown away something important?

_____

2. What would you do if you went on a safari?

_____

3. Have you ever been to a jazz concert?

_____

4. What would you rather do this Saturday — relax at home or go to a theme park?

_____

9 **Write.** Imagine you are taking a holiday to outer space. Write a paragraph about it. Use words and phrases from the box.

| as . . . as   because of   going to   if   might   would rather |

_____

_____

_____

_____

GAME

Read and write. Complete each sentence. Then find the mystery message.

1. An insect is ☐☐☐☐☐☐☐☐ ☐☐ the bad smell of certain plants.
   ₁

2. Because ☐☐ all your practising, you played that melody perfectly!
   ₂

3. Some animals have spots ☐☐☐☐ ☐☐☐☐ their predators.
   ₃ ₄

4. If he knew how to play the guitar, we ☐☐☐☐ ask him to be in our band.
   ₅

5. We go to the beach ☐☐☐☐ ☐☐☐☐☐ than I would like. I'd go every day if I could!
   ₆ ₇

6. I ☐☐☐☐☐ ☐☐☐☐☐☐ go to the beach than to a theme park.
   ₈

7. ☐☐☐☐☐☐ came to see you yesterday, but I don't know who it was.
   ₉

8. Dad thought that we ☐☐☐☐☐ go to see the ruins in Greece.
   _{10 11}

Mystery message:

☐☐☐☐☐ ☐☐☐☐☐☐ ☐☐☐☐☐☐☐☐☐☐☐ ,
1 2 5 8 7 8 7 3 6 6 1 10 9 4 7 6 6 10 11 7 9 4

☐☐☐☐☐ ☐☐☐ ?
3 8 7 9 4 1 2 5

47